This book belongs to:

____

2